ONE-STITCH STITCHERY

LITTLE
CRAFT BOOK
SERIES

By MADELEINE APPELL

Drawings by MILLICENT TRIKAMINAS

79- 9- 2

STERLING PUBLISHING CO., INC. **NEW YORK**

Oak Tree Press Co., Ltd. London & Sydney

Little Craft Book Series

Aluminum and Copper Tooling
Animating Films without a Camera
Appliqué and Reverse Appliqué
Balsa Wood Modelling
Bargello Stitchery
Beads Plus Macramé
Beauty Recipes from Natural Foods
Big-Knot Macramé
Candle-Making
Ceramics by Coil
Ceramics by Slab
Corn-Husk Crafts
Corrugated Carton Crafting
Costumes from Crepe Paper
Crafting with Nature's Materials
Creating from Remnants
Creating Silver Jewelry with Beads
Creating with Beads
Creating with Flexible Foam
Creating with Sheet Plastic
Creative Lace-Making with Thread and Yarn
Cross Stitchery
Decoupage—Simple and Sophisticated

Embossing of Metal (Repoussage)
Felt Crafting
Finger Weaving: Indian Braiding
Flower Pressing
Folding Table Napkins
Greeting Cards You Can Make
Hooked and Knotted Rugs
Horseshoe-Nail Crafting
Ideas for Collage
Inkle Loom Weaving
Junk Sculpture
Lacquer and Crackle
Leathercrafting
Macramé
Making Paper Flowers
Making Picture Frames
Making Shell Flowers
Masks
Metal and Wire Sculpture
Model Boat Building
Monster Masks
Nail Sculpture

Needlepoint Simplified
Net-Making and Knotting
Off-Loom Weaving
Organic Jewelry You Can Make
Patchwork and Other Quilting
Pictures without a Camera
Pin Pictures with Wire & Thread
Puppet-Making
Repoussage
Scissorscraft
Scrimshaw
Sculpturing with Wax
Sewing without a Pattern
Starting with Papier Mâché
Starting with Stained Glass
Stone Grinding and Polishing
Stringcraft
String Designs
String Things You Can Create
Tissue Paper Creations
Tole Painting
Whittling and Wood Carving

Dedication

To my parents, Harriet and Al Arbett, for giving me the spirit to create.

Acknowledgments

To Millicent Trikaminas for her companionship and help throughout the writing of the book.
To my husband, Stephen, special thanks for all his help, concern and love.

Copyright © 1978 by Madeleine Appell
Published by Sterling Publishing Co., Inc.
Two Park Avenue, New York, N.Y. 10016
Distributed in Australia and New Zealand by Oak Tree Press Co., Ltd.,
P.O. Box J34, Brickfield Hill, Sydney 2000, N.S.W.
Distributed in the United Kingdom and elsewhere in the British Commonwealth
by Ward Lock Ltd., 116 Baker Street, London W 1
Manufactured in the United States of America
All rights reserved
Library of Congress Catalog Card No.: 78-51063
Sterling ISBN 0-8069-5384-5 Trade   Oak Tree 7061-2587-8
5385-3 Library

Contents

Couching (see page 29).

Before You Begin 4

Tools and Materials 5

The Satin Stitch 11

The Running Stitch 20

Couching 25

The Roumanian Stitch 31

The Outline Stitch 34

The Cross Stitch 37

The Chain Stitch 40

The Split Stitch 42

The Blanket Stitch 44

The French Knot 46

Index 48

Before You Begin

There are few things more useful than the stitch. From our earliest ancestors who used needles of bone threaded with hair or dried grasses and sewed animal hides or bark to make the first garments, to today when home sewing machines are more or less commonplace, the stitch has been a basis of civilized life.

As the utilitarian aspects of sewing began to be mastered, the artist in man started to explore the creative possibilities of needle and thread. Embroidery soon became an important expression of these creative impulses, bringing about a marriage between functionalism and beauty. Embroidery was used to decorate clothing, linens, carpets, hangings and ecclesiastical garments. Sometimes it was used to record important events. The famous medieval Bayeux tapestry, for example, records the story of the Norman Conquest of England in 1066.

Embroidery was a vital art in such diverse ancient cultures as those of Egypt, Greece and the Orient. It also flourished in the Western Hemisphere, as long as 2000 years ago when the Nazca Indians of the south coastal valleys of the Andes were producing embroidered textiles in a remarkable range of hues.

Much modern embroidery is machine made. However, hand embroidery has become very popular in recent years, ranging from simple designs to complex and beautiful works of art. The variety of possibilities and techniques in embroidery today makes stitchery an art form accessible to all.

The vocabulary of the stitch is the same whether hemming a skirt or creating a stitched design. It is the way that vocabulary is used that makes the difference. Hemming a skirt is to a stitchery design what painting a wall is to painting a picture—the tools may be the same, but the results are unrelated. Artists work by exploring their tools and materials to find their own unique ways of handling them. It is with just this spirit that you should approach the vocabulary of stitches contained in this book.

Why One Stitch at a Time?

To give each stitch its due and master it, you must explore its full range of possibilities—how you can use it texturally, to make shapes, to create lightness and/or looseness, evenness and/or unevenness.

There are many embroidery stitches, but this book only introduces you to 10 of the most popular and commonly used ones. Each project teaches you one stitch and its standard variations. Thus, you can familiarize yourself with each individual stitch and its unique characteristics. Once you have mastered a stitch and the variations presented, you will be able to go on to explore, discover and invent others.

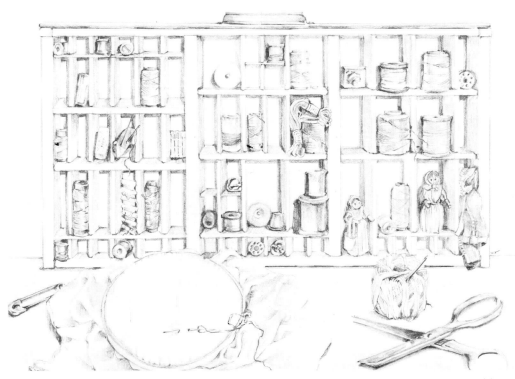

Illus. 1. Keeping your stitchery tools and materials in an open-faced cabinet such as this one can be a constant source of inspiration for you.

Tools and Materials

The first thing you need to do is gather your equipment. Stitchery tools and materials are quite simple and inexpensive. Many of them are common household items. There is more elaborate equipment available, but it is not essential for the basic stitchery you will learn here. The advantage of this art form is that you can easily arrange the equipment and work space you need in your home.

Keep your equipment separate from other sewing supplies so that it is always in perfect working condition and readily available.

Tools

Needles

TYPES AND CHARACTERISTICS	USES
1. *Crewel or embroidery*: sharp point; medium length; long eye; sizes: 1–10	wool thread; tightly woven fabric
2. *Tapestry*: blunt point; medium length; long eye; sizes: 13–24	any type of thread; loosely woven fabric such as burlap
3. *Sharp*: very sharp point; medium length; small eye; sizes: 5–12	cotton thread, single strand embroidery thread; tightly woven fabrics
4. *Chenille*: sharp point; short length; large eye; sizes: 18–22	thick threads such as tapestry wool; all fabrics

Other needles: upholstery, candlewick.

Scissors

Any household scissors will do if they have short, narrow blades with sharp points (manicuring scissors are a good example). The points must close perfectly so that they cut threads quickly and cleanly. You can buy embroidery scissors at any sewing notions shop.

Thimbles

Although a thimble is not necessary, many people sew more comfortably with one. A metal thimble is the best. Use it on the middle finger of your sewing hand.

Embroidery Hoops

A hoop or frame is necessary in stitchery to minimize puckering and to keep the fabric from twisting off the grain. Hoops are made of wood and metal and come in two parts: an inside circle and an outside circle that is either plain or has a metal thumb screw. The material is held taut between the two layers. A hoop with a thumb screw is better as it gives you more control over your material. Hoops range in size from 3 inches (7.5 cm.) to $13\frac{1}{2}$ inches (about 34 cm.) in diameter. A large-sized hoop is more practical as it is adaptable to a larger variety of work.

There are two types of hoops:

Hand-held: This hoop allows you to work comfortably in your lap and is, of course, portable.
Hoop on a stand: This hoop frees both hands for working. Stands vary in length from table stands

to floor models. A floor stand is adjustable for height and angle.

Embroidery Frames

When you are planning to work on a large piece, a frame is preferable to a hoop. Commercially made hand-held and floor frames are available. Both have mechanisms for rolling the fabric at the top and bottom of the frame if the fabric is larger than the frame. The floor frame has a pedestal that can adjust the height and angle of the frame. As with the hoop, the floor frame frees your hands to work on your stitchery.

If you do not want to invest in these mechanisms, there are two simple ways to construct a frame at home:

Picture frame: You can use any picture frame that is reasonably sturdy. Simply tack or staple the embroidery fabric to the frame.

Stretcher strips: You can buy stretcher strips pre-cut in a variety of sizes at any art supply shop. They have grooves at each end which allow the corners to fit together easily. Again, tack or staple the fabric to the frame.

Fabrics

Fabrics are a vital part of a stitchery painting. The texture and color of the fabric can enhance or complement the stitchery design. Once you have prepared a design, you should carefully choose the fabric for its color, its texture and its suitability for the types of threads you plan to use. The fabric need not be solid in color. Sometimes a print, gingham, or pillow ticking can become a part of the stitchery design.

FABRIC	USES
1. *Linen*: medium weight, even weave	counted thread work *(cross stitch)*
2. *Cotton and cotton blends*: includes homespun, denim, sailcloth, hopsacking, muslin	solid work; anything requiring a sturdy fabric
3. *Burlap*: very loose weave; highly textured	free, bold work; earthy textural effects
4. *Wool*: smooth finish; loosely woven	fine work; loose work; very flexible; can be delicate or textural
5. *Silk*: smooth, tight weave; shiny	delicate, subtle effects

6. *Felt, pellon*:
   non-woven, smooth   flat work, good for couching

Other fabrics: suede, monk's cloth, upholstery and drapery fabrics, corduroy, crepe, chiffon, knits, polyester, buckram, onion sacking, screening (metal or plastic).

Threads

The three characteristics of thread to consider are color, texture and weight. There is a tremendous range of colors available, as well as a variety of unusual textures and weights. The texture of thread affects its color so that a bright red cotton and a bright red wool are not exactly the same color. Weight and texture create three-dimensional and other special visual effects unique to stitchery. Consider, for instance, the exquisite lustre you can achieve if you use silk or shiny cotton thread. The choice of threads and colors is, indeed, an extremely important and exciting part in the working out of your stitchery designs.

TYPES OF THREAD   APPEARANCE

1. *Cotton.* Cotton is available in a large variety of colors and weights. Its three types are:

A. *Floss*:
   fine; six-stranded; may be divided into one-,   polished surface, flat
   two- and three-strand groupings

B. *Pearl*:
   twisted thread; cannot be divided; common   glossy, textural
   sizes: #3, #5, #8

C. *Crochet*:
   similar to pearl, but not twisted   semi-glossy
   Note: You can also use ordinary cotton sewing thread, sizes 40, 60, 80, 100.

2. *Wool.*
A. *Crewel*:
    lightly twisted two-ply worsted yarn; can be   textured
    separated into single strands

B. *Tapestry*:
    lightly twisted; strong   smooth

C. *Knitting worsted*:
    very loosely twisted   smooth

Other wools: rug yarn, hand spun, synthetics.

3. *Silk floss.*
    stranded and twisted   glossy

4. *Cords and twine.*
    Not ordinarily thought of as embroidery   coarse, uneven thickness
    threads, these add interesting and unusual
    textures to a design.

A. *Jute*:
    thick, several ply   rough

B. *Wrapping twine*:
    thinner than jute; natural colors only

Storage

Work space that is well organized and pleasant to be in makes a productive setting for an artist. Your work place can be anything from a drawer for storage and the kitchen table to an entire room set apart for the purpose. Only a few things are important: that your storage area be organized and used only for stitchery tools and materials, that the work space be well lit and that the work table be at a comfortable height.

Tools

Keep your tools in an enclosed space which has compartments for separating needles, scissors, thimbles and small hoops. Store this tool box in a drawer and bring it to the work area when you are ready to sew.

Keep your needles in a pin cushion, thrust in as deeply as possible to avoid exposure to the air, or on cards or felt that you can fold for the same reason. You can store hoops and frames in order of size in a flat box or on a closet shelf. Pencils, drawing paper, carbon paper and tracing paper should also be available somewhere near the work area.

Fabrics

The best way to store fabric is to roll it around a cardboard tube. This prevents creases. If you must fold the fabric, avoid leaving it folded the same way for too long. Open it and re-fold it several times a year. Store fabric out of direct sunlight which will fade it. Closed bins, drawers or closets make the best storage places.

Thread

Thread can accumulate at an alarming rate when you begin working on stitcheries. After each project, you are bound to have some thread left over. Store left-over threads by wrapping them around a cardboard tube, taping the ends. Store threads by color and type in clear boxes or on a shelf, in a drawer or hung on a wall.

Once you have gathered and organized your tools and materials, you are ready to begin stitching. One important rule to remember before you start is that a simple design based on *your* ideas and experiences is more rewarding to stitch than one you have simply copied. Use the projects in this book as learning tools and inspiration; then create your own unique stitcheries using the techniques you have mastered.

The Satin Stitch

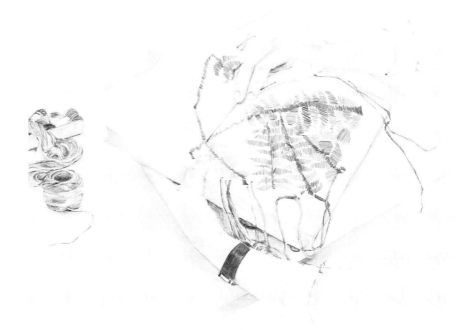

Illus. 2. Solid shapes, such as the fern leaves in this design, lend themselves well to the satin stitch.

The *satin stitch* is a simple, flat stitch. Because you make the stitches close together and with even tension, a satiny appearance results. The *surface* or *sham satin stitch* looks like the *satin stitch*, but conserves thread because you only work on the surface of the fabric.

The *satin stitch* can be used to create solid shapes such as structures, figures, animals and leaves.

Planning the Design

The first thing you must do is choose a design for your stitchery. Possible subject matter for embroideries are landscapes (including seascapes and cityscapes), still-lifes, figures, portraits or abstracts. Look around you for artistic themes. Even ordinary objects take on special qualities when stitched.

When planning designs for your stitchery paintings, keep in mind that some stitches are more appropriate for certain subjects, themes, textures and patterns than others. Also, the needle, the main stitchery tool, is not as flexible as some other artists' tools. Do not expect to reproduce life-like images exactly, or to stitch true-to-life shading. Instead, you will have to work from

Illus. 4. Using a rectangular paper frame, choose which area of the object you would like to stitch.

Illus. 3. To utilize the close-up device to create a stitchery design, first select an attractive or interesting object, such as this fern plant, to zero in on.

sketches, photographs, your imagination and other sources mentioned throughout this book, and then adapt your ideas for your stitchery.

Begin with a simple design, so you can concentrate on the basic techniques and procedures rather than on an intricate pattern. The subject chosen for the *satin stitch* creation in Illus. 5 is the leaves of a fern plant. The device used to create this design is called the *close-up*, a term taken from film terminology. The close-up is a way of zeroing in on a small area of a large object. You might want to use this method to eliminate extra detail, or to concentrate on one area of a subject that is more interesting than the whole thing.

You can use the close-up method of choosing a design either with a photograph or with an actual object. Cut a rectangle out of a piece of paper to use as a frame. Hold the frame up to the subject and move it around until it encloses an interesting composition. See Illus. 3 and 4. Now sketch the final composition onto a piece of canvas or drawing paper to use as a pattern.

Preparing the Fabric

Scaling

After you have a design, choose a suitable background fabric for your stitchery (see page 7). An even-wool fabric was used for the fern project. The fabric measured 15 inches × 15 inches (37.5 cm. × 37.5 cm.). Since the fern close-up only measured 9 inches × 9 inches (22.5 cm. × 22.5 cm.), scaling was necessary to enlarge it.

Illus. 5. Using realistic colors in a variety of different weight threads resulted in this lush fern picture done in the satin stitch.

If your original drawing or design is larger or smaller than the planned stitchery, you will need scaling to reduce or enlarge it.

Using pencil or chalk, draw a grid on the original design. The simplest way to do this is to draw two lines, one vertical and one horizontal, through the mid-point of the design, creating four equal boxes. If you want, you can draw additional, equally spaced vertical and horizontal lines.

Then repeat this process on tracing paper or directly on the stitchery fabric. For this piece, the design was repeated directly on the fabric. Now re-draw the design onto the second grid, carefully transferring the designs from the appropriate boxes.

Stretcher Frame Method

For this stitchery, 12-inch × 12-inch (30-cm. × 30-cm.) stretcher strips were used. Always cut an additional 2 inches (5 cm.) of fabric for a border to stretch over the wood if you use stretchers.

Center the fabric on the face of the stretcher frame. Wrap the fabric around to the back of the stretchers. Staple the fabric to the stretchers.

Choosing the Thread

Use thread whose colors and textures complement your chosen design. If you are making the fern stitchery in Illus. 5, pick realistic colors—use a broad range of greens, blue-greens, yellows and yellow-golds for the leaves and several shades of brown for the stems. Using a variety of single- or double-ply threads—from cotton floss to wools —added special texture to the creation in Illus. 5. Use a sharp-pointed medium-length needle if you use these threads.

Stitching

Before you actually begin a project, it is a good idea to practice the instructions for each stitch on a piece of scrap fabric. First thread the needle and make a knot. Use a length of thread approximately 30 inches (75 cm.) long for any embroidery you do.

Satin Stitch (Illus. 6)

Step 1: Bring the needle up from the back of the fabric.

Step 2: Place the needle down into the fabric a short distance from where you brought the needle up in Step 1.

Step 3: Repeat Steps 1 and 2. Begin the next stitch as close to the first stitch as possible. It is very important to keep the tension consistent throughout when you do the *satin stitch*.

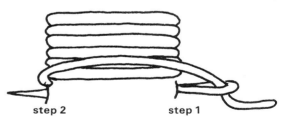

step 2   step 1

Illus. 6. The satin stitch.

Variations

1. Follow the instructions above, but vary the length of the stitches to conform to a specific shape (see Illus. 7).

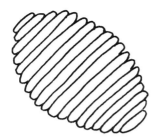

Illus. 7. Variation 1 of the satin stitch.

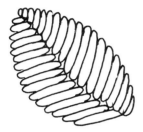

Illus. 8. Variation 2 of the satin stitch.

Illus. 9. This fern stitchery was worked by jumping freely from one area to another. This is a good way to get an advance idea of how your final creation will look.

2. Follow the instructions above, but change the directions of the stitches within a given shape (see Illus. 8).

Method of Stitching

Begin by working one area of your design. You may continue in any of the following manners: work one area at a time; work one color at a time; work one type of thread at a time; jump around freely from area to area. In any case, keep the original design handy for easy reference.

This particular *satin stitch* piece was worked by jumping around freely from one area to another, as you can see in Illus. 9.

Finishing and Mounting

After you have completed stitching, you must then decide how to finish your creation. The texture, design, color, emphasis and feeling of your stitchery should help you determine how you want to complete your project.

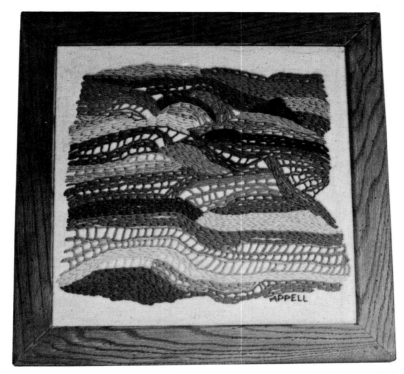

Illus. 10. A photograph of mountains and hills inspired this beautiful stitchery, which was done in the chain stitch and its variations. See page 40 for instructions.

Illus. 11. This simple, yet graceful, bird was done in the split stitch and its variations. Instructions for this interesting picture begin on page 42.

Illus. 12. Embroidery stitches are really quite versatile, as you can tell by comparing this free-form split-stitch creation with the bird in Illus. 11. By using different threads—cords and jute, as well as thick wools, were used here—you can completely change the feeling you evoke with any particular stitch.

Illus. 13. Here is another example of the type of work you can do using the satin stitch. Simplifying the human figures into geometric shapes prepared this dance rehearsal scene for stitching.

Before mounting any stitchery, make sure it is flat (iron or steam it if necessary). Trim any frayed edges and secure dangling threads on the back by anchoring them under other threads.

The No-Frame Method

Some stitchery paintings are complete in themselves and actually do not need a frame. This is true particularly of a design that has large open spaces and is done on a heavily textured fabric. The fern stitchery in Illus. 5 is a good example of this. Simply stretching the work over wood or cardboard is a sufficient finishing. You can easily stretch the stitchery over stretcher strips, and staple the fabric to the back. If you worked this piece on stretcher strips, nothing extra is required for finishing. Simply hammer a nail into the wall and hang up your creation.

Another stitchery being done in the *satin stitch* is in Illus. 13. The subject is ballet dancers in rehearsal. The design was prepared for stitching using simplification, a commonly used technique in stitchery. Simplification is a means of reducing objects to their basic shapes. Almost any subject you choose can be very interesting if you simplify it. Even quite complex forms, such as the human

Illus. 14. This drawing of rehearsing dancers was the original design for the stitchery begun in Illus. 13.

Illus. 15. This is the same drawing as in Illus. 14, but the shapes have been simplified for stitching.

figure, can be broken down into simple shapes to make stitching it easier. First, eliminate all extraneous detail. Then, reduce the form or forms to their nearest geometric equivalents. (For example, flowers become a series of concentric circles or simple elongated ovals, and the human body becomes cubes, ovals, circles or combina-

tions of these shapes.) See Illus. 15 for the simplified dance rehearsal.

Use the same procedure as described for the fern for preparing and stitching this piece. Illus. 13 is being done in black, white and grey six-stranded cotton embroidery floss. You can, of course, use any colors you wish.

The Running Stitch

The *running stitch* is a simple running in and out with the needle through the cloth. Probably the first stitch ever used, it is the basis of all other stitches.

You can use the *running stitch* to stitch buildings, bricks, stones, lettering, or any other shape where you want open spaces. The *running stitch* creates a flat, even surface, somewhat textured in appearance because of the spaces in-between the stitches.

Planning the Design

The subject for the *running-stitch* design in Illus. 16 is letters. The design was worked out as a colored construction paper collage.

Collage

The word "collage" comes from the French verb meaning to paste. A collage is a work of art made

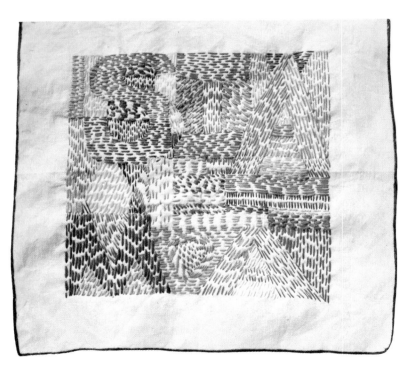

Illus. 16. A collage made from a variety of construction-paper letters formed the design for this running-stitch master-piece, which was stitched on a large linen napkin. Why not make a set of personalized napkins to give as a unique gift?

by pasting down different types of papers, fabrics, or other two-dimensional textures onto a background, such as a board or canvas. For a stitchery, simply work with colored construction paper, shiny paper, newspaper or fabrics to make a pleasing arrangement of the materials. Then, try to visualize each different type of texture as a different color and/or texture of thread.

Preparing the Fabric

Illus. 16 was stitched on a large linen napkin. If you make your collage the exact size of the planned stitchery, scaling is not necessary. Use the tissue-paper method to transfer your collage design to the fabric.

Tissue-Paper Method of Transfer

Trace your collage design onto a piece of tissue paper. Carefully secure the tissue-paper drawing to the fabric with pins. Using thin cotton thread, sew *running stitches* (see instructions following) along the outline of your design. Tear the tissue paper away from the fabric when you have transferred the entire design. This method works best with loosely woven, heavily textured fabrics.

Choosing the Thread

In making this piece, choose colors according to your collage model. Use contrasting colors in shapes which are adjacent to each other. Blues, reds, oranges, yellows, browns and greens make up the color scheme of Illus. 16. Cotton—floss and pearl, and wool—crewel, tapestry, and knitting worsted—were used for this work. Use several

Illus. 17. A fabric collage made from abstract shapes is a fun type of original design that you can create. You can then adapt your patterned collage and embroider it, using one of the stitches and its variations you will learn in this book.

sizes of sharp needles if you use this same variety of threads.

Stitching

For this piece, use a small hand-held hoop. Remember to practice the *running stitch* on a scrap of fabric before you begin to stitch your final design.

Running Stitch (Illus. 18)

The *running stitch* is a simple running in and out of the fabric. This forms a row of uniform stitches with uniform spaces between them.

Step 1: Put the needle down through the fabric.

Step 2: Bring the needle up through the fabric a short distance from where you put the needle down into the fabric.

Step 3: Continue stitching in and out in a straight line.

Variations

1. Follow the instructions above, but vary the length of the spaces in-between the stitches (see Illus. 19).

Illus. 19. Variation 1 of the running stitch.

2. Follow the instructions above, but vary the direction of the rows within a specific shape (see Illus. 20).

step 1
step 2

Illus. 18. The running stitch.

Illus. 20. Variation 2 of the running stitch.

Method of Stitching

For this piece, work one area at a time. Simply move the hoop from one area to another as you stitch.

Finishing and Mounting

After you have finished stitching, prepare your project for framing as described on page 18. Then consider how you want to frame your creation. A frame can serve as part of the work itself or merely as an accent. Consider a frame's width, weight, color and texture. Also consider the question of a border: your stitchery may look best with a border of its own background fabric or framed flush to the ends of the design itself.

Frames are available in wood, metal and plastic, and come ready-made in standard sizes or cut to size by a professional framer. A plastic frame was used for Illus. 16. The advantage of a professional framer is that he has plastic frames in color. The ready-made plastic frames are all clear plastic. If you want, you can choose a clear plastic box which comes in standard sizes. Although your stitchery will look unframed, the box serves as a protective covering for your work. Also, you do not have to mount the stitchery to enclose it in a box. Simply tape the fabric around the back of the inner part of the box and then place the cover over it. Illus. 21 shows the plastic box used for this project.

Stitchery Sculpture

Illus. 22 is an example of an abstract design worked in the *running stitch* and then shaped into a truly unique soft sculpture.

Plan an abstract design on a piece of paper or cardboard. Then transfer this pattern to a clean, solid-colored pillow-case. Using dressmaker's carbon paper is the easiest way to do this. You can buy dressmaker's carbon paper at a sewing supply shop. Choose a color which contrasts with the pillow-case. Secure the carbon paper to the pillow-case with pins. Place your design on the carbon paper and trace over it with a tracing wheel. This method is most successful with flat, even-weave fabrics.

Now, stitch carefully to avoid going through both layers of the pillow-case. Then stuff the pillow-case using 100 per cent polyester fibre. Sew the pillow-case closed. Following the forms suggested by the stitched design, fold, crease and pucker the stuffed pillow-case. Tack down the resulting forms with matching colored thread. Display this stitchery sculpture as you would any other sculpture.

Illus. 22 (above). As you can see from this unique soft sculpture, whose design was created with the running stitch, stitchery projects do not have to be hung on a wall. This fascinating object was transformed from a plain pillow-case into this one-of-a-kind sculpture.

Illus. 23 (right). This fabulously textured landscape with a setting sun clearly demonstrates the kind of powerful stitcheries you can create using the blanket stitch and its variations. The instructions begin on page 44.

Couching

Couching has been traced back as far as Scythian embroideries of the first century B.C. It was also used in German and Swiss embroideries worked in convents from the 15th to the 17th centuries. The stitch was developed to use with delicate threads (such as metallic threads) which would be damaged if pulled through the ground material or for heavy threads which were too thick to pull through.

Illus. 24 (above). One of the most textured stitches is the French knot, which was used to stitch this unusual still-life. The roundness of the subject matter suggested a round frame, so the piece was simply left in its wooden embroidery hoop for hanging.

Illus. 25 (right). Striking colors and a very textured surface characterize this beautiful example of couching. A cut-up onion inspired the circular motif, perfect for this stitch.

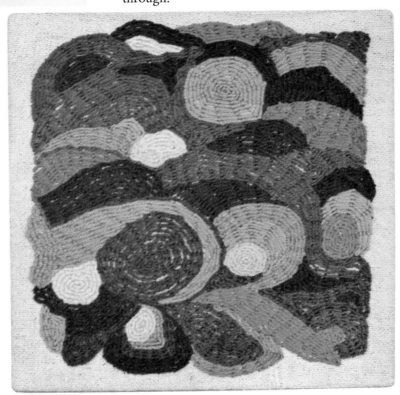

Choose a shape or shapes. On a piece of paper the same size as your planned stitchery, make an artistic arrangement based on the repetition of that shape. You may vary the size of the shape, change its direction, overlap or use only a part of the shape in working out a unique composition. Remember that the spaces between the shapes will also be an important part of your design.

Illus. 26. As you can see, the interesting lines inside a cut-up onion offer artistic possibilities for stitchery designs.

Couching can be used to create abstract patterns, circular shapes, lines, grille-work or gates. It has a flat texture with a slightly raised surface at specific intervals.

Planning the Design

The subject for the striking *couching stitch* creation in Illus. 25 is an onion. The design resulted from a technique called repetition.

To compose a pattern using repetition, you simply repeat specific lines or shapes you have chosen. Some sources for interesting shapes are: nature—leaves, petals, water patterns; household objects—keys, kitchen or workshop tools or furniture; abstract forms—certain items, such as letters or numbers, have inherent design qualities and adapt well to this technique.

Illus. 27. Repeating the simple lines from the cut-up onion resulted in the design shown here.

Preparing the Fabric

Stretcher strips were used for this project (see page 14). An even-weave cotton fabric the same size as the planned design was used, so scaling was unnecessary.

Transfer your planned design to the fabric using the carbon-paper technique described on page 23. Staple the fabric to the stretchers.

Choosing the Thread

For this piece, three-ply tapestry wool in several shades of green, blue-green and yellow was used. Of course, you can use any colors you wish to stitch your repetitive design. Use a length of whatever thread you choose that is 30 inches (75 cm.) long.

Stitching

Couching (Illus. 28)

Couching is simply a means of sewing down a thread or threads on the surface of the fabric using a single *tacking stitch* at right angles to the direction of the main thread.

Step 1: Place the thread to be couched on the fabric.

Step 2: Coming up from the back of the fabric, take a stitch at right angles to the laid thread, crossing over the thread and tacking it down.

Step 3: Repeat Step 2 at regular intervals.

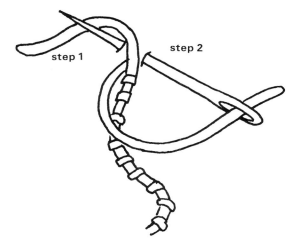

Illus. 28. Couching.

Variations

1. Follow the instructions above, but vary the spaces between the *tacking stitches* (see Illus. 29).

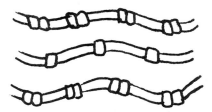

Illus. 29. Variation 1 of couching.

2. Follow the instructions above, but tack down more than one thread at a time (see Illus. 30).

Illus. 30. Variation 2 of couching.

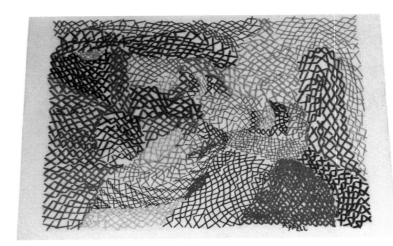

Illus. 31. The cross stitch and its variations resulted in this marvellous mixture of densely filled areas and open, lacy spaces. The nature of this stitch is such that the spaces in-between the crosses become an important part of the over-all effect. Instructions for this work of art begin on page 37.

Illus. 32. This graceful and flowing seascape was also made using the cross stitch. Although this stitch is often used for lettering, you can see that by varying the size and shape of the crosses you can create smooth and rolling waves.

Illus. 33. Even ordinary household objects can become the basis for stitcheries. This magnificent piece was inspired by a part of a chair! Couching in a variety of colors was used to execute the design.

Method of Stitching

The design in Illus. 25 was worked one area at a time.

Finishing and Mounting

This project was completed like the *satin stitch* fern picture on page 18.

Abstracting

Abstracting is another way to create an original design. This technique was used for Illus. 33, another work made with the *couching stitch*. A photograph of a chair prompted this stitchery (see Illus. 34 and 35). Here again, you can work from life, a photograph or a drawing. Find an unusual, interesting and attractive area within a larger subject. Block it off by drawing a frame around it or by using the frame technique described on page

13. Now, draw that segment onto a small area of your chosen background fabric. Extend the lines suggested by the fragment until they touch the outer edges of the fabric. Add any additional lines that echo the shapes of the original small section or the new shapes suggested by the extended lines.

Follow the same procedures as above to make a stitchery design after you are pleased with your pattern.

Illus. 34. Some of the intricate lines in this chair became the basis of the pattern used for Illus. 33.

Illus. 35. After the artist singled out the specific part of the chair she wanted to abstract for this piece, she then extended the lines as shown here to complete the design.

The Roumanian Stitch

The *Roumanian stitch* dates back to early 18th-century American crewel work. It is said to be one of the basic stitches used for quilts, coverlets and curtains. *Janina stitch*, *Oriental couching* and *antique couching* are other names for this stitch and its variations.

The *Roumanian stitch* creates a rough, raised surface with uneven heights. It is, therefore, perfect for depicting such things as landscapes, leaves, trees or waves.

Planning the Design

Rose petals inspired the *Roumanian stitch* piece shown in color Illus. 38. Using repetition (see page 26), the artist created a circular design which became the natural border for the picture. If your original drawing is not the same size as your planned stitchery, change its size as described on page 14.

Preparing the Fabric

Linen fabric was used for Illus. 38, which was worked on a medium-sized wooden embroidery hoop. If you use this type of hoop, be sure to cut the fabric approximately 4 inches (10 cm.) larger than the actual size of the stitchery. Use a hoop that is larger than the planned design. This way, you can position the hoop around the design and leave it in that position until you have completed the work.

Choosing the Thread

Illus. 38 was made from various shades of crewel wool—green, red, yellow and blue. If you choose crewel wool for your stitchery, use a crewel needle. Use a 30-inch (75-cm.) length of thread.

Stitching

Roumanian Stitch (Illus. 36 and 37)

The *Roumanian stitch* is similar to the *satin stitch*, but it is tied down with a smaller, slanting stitch usually in the middle of the longer stitch.

Step 1: Starting from the back of the fabric, make a simple stitch any length you want.

Step 2: Bring the needle through from the back at the middle, below the first stitch.

Step 3: Cross over the first stitch on the diagonal and pull the stitch flat.

Step 4: Repeat Steps 1 to 3.

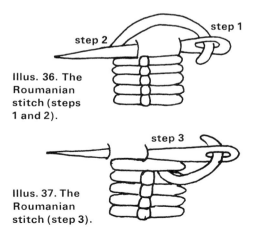

Illus. 36. The Roumanian stitch (steps 1 and 2).

Illus. 37. The Roumanian stitch (step 3).

31

79-9-2

Chrome, brass and silver are the most popular types of metal frames. Although a professional framer can supply metal framing, there is a wide selection of ready-made metal frames available. These are easy to put together and are considerably less expensive than custom-made frames. Using a metal frame is a simple, but handsome way of finishing off a stitchery.

Another stitchery done in the *Roumanian stitch* is shown in Illus. 40. Crewel wool was used throughout this colorful landscape with trees.

Illus. 38. Rose petals formed the idea for this circular Roumanian-stitch project. The use of contrasting colors makes this a particularly striking creation.

Variations

1. Follow the instructions above, but vary the length of each stitch and the placement of the *tacking stitch* (see Illus. 39).
2. Follow the instructions above, but curve the stitches (see Illus. 41).

Method of Stitching

One area at a time was worked to stitch the rose-inspired design in Illus. 38.

Finishing and Mounting

After you have ironed your stitchery, choose a frame. A metal frame was chosen for Illus. 38.

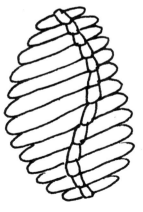

Illus. 39. Variation 1 of the Roumanian stitch.

Illus. 40. Outstanding colors and incredible texture characterize this magnificent Roumanian-stitch landscape. Covering the entire background with this raised stitch resulted in the appropriate earthiness of the work.

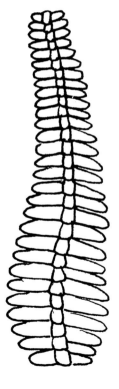

Illus. 41. Variation 2 of the Roumanian stitch.

The Outline Stitch

The *outlinestitch*, frequently used by 17th-century embroiderers, was first taught at what is now the Royal School of Needlework in London. It is also known as the *crewel, stem, stalk,* or *South Kensington stitch.*

As its name indicates, the *outline stitch* is often used for outlining. However, you can also use it to stitch abstract shapes or in places where you need a solid area of color, such as rocks, tree bark, rope or leaves. Its characteristic delicate line is also suitable for grass. The *outline stitch* creates a rippling, raised surface. It looks flatter when the stitches are elongated and higher when the stitches are wider.

Planning the Design

A collage made from magazine photographs was the design for the planned stitchery in Illus.

42. To create this type of collage, choose several photographs that are related by color, shapes, subject matter, patterns of light and dark, or mood. Rip or cut out the photographs and arrange them on a board or piece of paper the same size as your planned stitchery. Fit the photograph parts together like a puzzle, side by side, overlapping or with spaces between. Continue to rearrange the pieces until you have worked out an interesting and attractive design.

The photographs for the collage in Illus. 43 were all outdoor country scenes with grass, trees and sky.

Preparing the Fabric

For Illus. 42 burlap fabric was stapled to stretcher strips. Because the collage was the same size as the planned stitchery, scaling was not necessary. Instead, the design was transferred to the burlap using the carbon-paper technique described on page 23.

Illus. 42. The outline stitch is being used here to stitch this rustic, outdoor scene. The stitch lends itself particularly well to grass, tree bark and leaves, all of which are central in this design.

Illus. 42. You will need various sizes of needles if you use a similar assortment of threads.

Illus. 43. An interesting and unusual collage resulted from a collection of photographs, all of which had an outdoor theme.

Choosing the Thread

If you based your design on a photograph collage, you might prefer to use threads which have realistic colors. Silks, cotton floss and wools in shades of green, brown and blue are being used in

Stitching

Thread the needle and make a knot. Use a length of thread approximately 30 inches (75 cm.) long.

Outline Stitch (Illus. 44 and 45)

Step 1: Make a simple, flat stitch.
Step 2: Take a *back stitch* with the needle coming out halfway along and just beside the first stitch.
Step 3: Repeat, making sure to keep the thread on the same side of the needle.

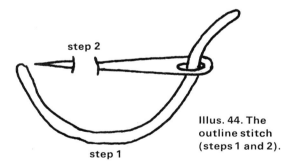

Illus. 44. The outline stitch (steps 1 and 2).

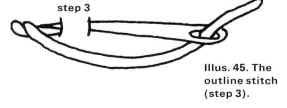

Illus. 45. The outline stitch (step 3).

35

Variations

1. Follow the instructions above, but make the line thinner by making the stitch longer (see Illus. 47).

2. Follow the instructions above, but make the line broader by picking up more cloth on both sides of the outline (see Illus. 48).

Method of Stitching

Illus. 42 is being worked freely, moving from section to section.

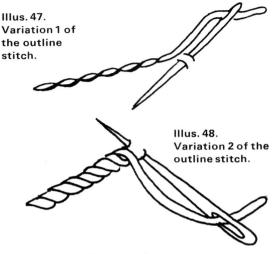

**Illus. 47.
Variation 1 of
the outline
stitch.**

**Illus. 48.
Variation 2 of the
outline stitch.**

Finishing and Mounting

Since this picture was worked on stretcher strips, you can simply finish it as described on page 18.

Another way of finishing and mounting a stitchery worked on stretcher strips is shown in the *outline-stitch* design in Illus. 46. Here, wood stripping completed the project. Wood stripping is a simple and very inexpensive way to frame a work. Stripping comes in various widths and thicknesses. You simply saw an appropriate length of stripping into four pieces to match the sides of the work. You can mitre the corners or leave them flat. Stain, varnish or paint each strip. Then nail each piece into place along each of the sides of the completed stitchery.

Illus. 46. Superb coloring and outstanding texture combine to make this outline-stitch picture a truly beautiful one.

The Cross Stitch

One of the oldest stitches, the *cross stitch* has appeared in embroideries all over the world. Although it is commonly associated with American samplers, the *cross stitch* is also frequently associated with peasant communities. Excellent examples of the *cross stitch* have been found in southeast Europe, India, Persia, the Near East and the Greek islands.

The *cross stitch* is usually done on loosely woven linen so that the stitches can be counted easily. It creates flat, even surfaces with a slight textural feeling due to the spaces between the stitches. Interesting patterns result from these in-between spaces as well as from the stitches themselves.

The *cross stitch* is often used for lettering, but may also be used for open work, gates, landscapes, water and trees in full bloom.

Planning the Design

The stitchery in color Illus. 31 originated as a collage made from several different types of fabric. Choose a variety of different colors and textures of fabric to create an unusual and unique piece.

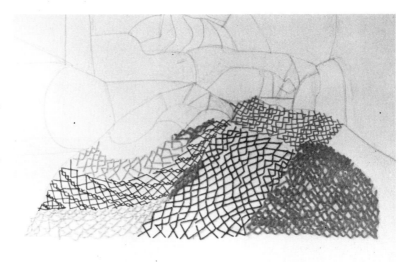

Illus. 49. Pieces of differently patterned fabrics, which comprised the original collage design for this project, are being re-interpreted on the background fabric as different sizes, densities and colors of cross stitches. The result is the attractive wall hanging shown in color Illus. 31.

Preparing the Fabric

For this stitchery, an even-weave cotton fabric was used.

Scaling was necessary because the collage was smaller than the planned stitchery. If your fabric collage is smaller than you want your stitchery to be, enlarge it and transfer it to your background fabric as described on page 14.

Staple the fabric to stretcher strips as described on page 14.

Choosing the Thread

Illus. 31 was stitched with various textures of thread to correspond to the different textures in the original fabric collage. Use several different-sized needles, depending on the types of threads you choose. Several shades of brown, red, orange and purple compose this striking picture.

Stitching

Thread the needle with a 30-inch (75 cm.) length of thread.

Cross Stitch (Illus. 50 and 51)

The *cross stitch* is composed of two diagonal stitches that cross at the middle.

Step 1: Make a row of diagonal stitches, leaving even spaces between the stitches.

Step 2: Come back along the original row, crossing the stitches from right to left.

Variations

1. Follow the instructions above, but change the position of each stitch (see Illus. 52).

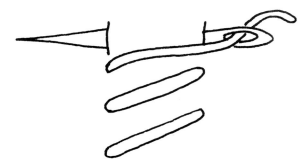

Illus. 50. The cross stitch (step 1).

2. Follow the instructions above, but cross the stitch above or below the middle (see Illus. 53).

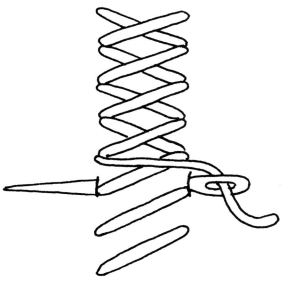

Illus. 51. The cross stitch (step 2).

Method of Stitching

Illus. 31 was done by stitching one area at a time. Notice in Illus. 31 that each section of *cross stitch* varies in density and size to create the desired textures from the collage. Keep the original design handy for easy reference.

Illus. 52. Variation 1 of the cross stitch.

Finishing and Mounting

Finish your *cross-stitch* embroidery using one of the methods you have learned.

Another *cross-stitch* design is pictured in Illus. 54. Several shades of blue, purple, red and yellow resulted in this lovely seascape. Six-strand cotton embroidery floss was used throughout.

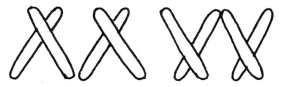

Illus. 53. Variation 2 of the cross stitch.

Illus. 54. The feeling of undulating waves is definitely evident as you look at this cross-stitched seascape. This lovely piece is also shown in color Illus. 32.

The Chain Stitch

The *chain stitch* is one of the oldest and most universally used stitches. It may be used to portray flowing hills, flower forms, large areas in landscapes, fish scales and ladders. It has an open, airy feeling and results in a slightly raised surface.

Planning the Design

A photograph of mountains and hills inspired Illus. 55 which was made in the *chain stitch*. The close-up design device described on page 12 was used to create this piece.

Illus. 55. Majestic mountains and hills—the subject of a photograph which inspired this stitchery —are definitely brought to mind by the varied chain stitches. This is also shown in color Illus. 10.

Preparing the Fabric

A commercial lap frame was used while stitching this piece onto monk's cloth. If you plan to use this type of frame, cut your piece of fabric 4 to 6 inches (10 to 15 cm.) larger than your planned design. Then, attach the fabric to the rollers following the specific instructions which came with your frame.

Next, transfer your pattern to the fabric. The carbon-paper method of transfer (see page 23) was used for Illus. 55, but you can use whatever method seems easiest to re-draw your particular design.

Choosing the Thread

Several thicknesses of wool in earthy tones of browns and purples resulted in the striking stitchery in Illus. 55. As always, choose colors and textures of wool which will enhance your design. Prepare a 30-inch (75-cm.) length of whatever thread you choose.

Stitching

Chain Stitch (Illus. 56 and 57)

Step 1: Bring the needle up from the back of the fabric.

Step 2: Form a loop on the surface of the fabric and hold it down with your thumb.

Step 3: Insert the needle just above where you first brought it up; then bring the point out a short distance below that.

Step 4: Pull the thread through, keeping the working thread under the needle point.

Step 5: Repeat Steps 1 to 4 as many times as you want.

Step 6: End a row with a small anchoring stitch.

Variations

1. Follow the instructions above, but elongate the stitches to create a thinner chain with less open space (see Illus. 58.)

2. Work Steps 1 and 2. Then insert the needle parallel to, but at a distance from, the original point. This results in an open chain (see Illus. 59 and 60).

Method of Stitching

For any *chain-stitch* sampler, work with one color of thread at a time.

Finishing and Mounting

Prepare your picture for framing as described on page 18. Illus. 55 was framed professionally in a wooden frame. Wooden frames are the most traditional and the most commonly used. Pine, oak, birch, cherry, and rosewood are only some of the many woods used for this purpose. You can leave a wooden frame natural, stain it, varnish it, antique it, or paint it. You may choose a smooth, rough, knotty, or weathered-look finish. Your choice, of course, depends upon which texture, color and width looks best with your stitchery. Always bring your stitchery along with you when going to choose a professionally-made frame.

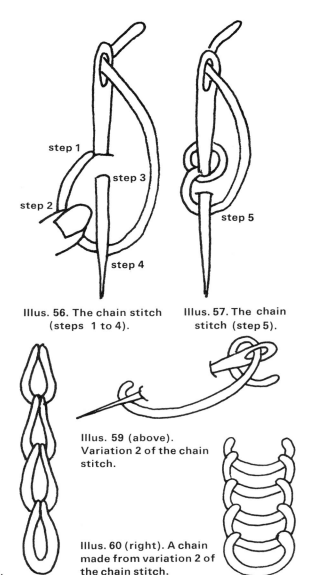

Illus. 56. The chain stitch (steps 1 to 4).

Illus. 57. The chain stitch (step 5).

Illus. 59 (above). Variation 2 of the chain stitch.

Illus. 60 (right). A chain made from variation 2 of the chain stitch.

Illus. 58. Variation 1 of the chain stitch.

41

The Split Stitch

The *split stitch* is closely related to the *chain stitch*, but has a character all its own. In the Middle Ages, it was used extensively for depicting hands and faces in embroidery, mostly on ecclesiastical furnishings.

The *split stitch* is used for linear designs and fine, detailed subjects such as hands, faces, flowers, curved forms and solid shapes.

The nature of this stitch is such that you only work it successfully using multiple-ply threads such as crewel, wool or embroidery floss. The result is rough and linear.

Planning the Design

A photograph of a bird reinterpreted in line resulted in the graceful *split-stitch* bird in Illus. 11.

To utilize this method of interpretation, you represent the shapes and shadows of an object by various densities of lines. This can actually be a simple but very graphic stylization of the original subject. Illus. 61 and 62 show the linear representation of the bird in Illus. 63 and color Illus. 11.

Preparing the Fabric

Stretcher strips were used for the even-weave linen chosen for this project. Scaling was not

Illus. 61. This is the original drawing of a bird made for a planned split-stitch project.

Illus. 62. The drawing was then translated into a linear representation which was, in turn, translated into split stitches.

Illus. 63. Here is the completed, stitched bird. This split-stitched creation is also shown in color Illus. 11.

necessary because the design was the exact size of the planned stitchery. The design was transferred to the fabric with dressmaker's carbon paper as described on page 23.

Choosing the Thread

Pick a different, contrasting color for each linear section of your design. Use both wool and cotton for variety in texture. You will need several different-sized needles depending on the threads' sizes.

Stitching

Thread the needle with a 30-inch (75-cm.) length of thread and make a knot.

Split Stitch (Illus. 64, 65, and 66)

Step 1: Make a simple, flat stitch.
Step 2: Make a *back stitch* with the needle coming out halfway back and through the previous stitch, thus piercing it with the needle.
Step 3: Repeat Steps 1 and 2.

Variations

1. Follow the instructions above, but vary the length of the stitches (see Illus. 67).
2. Follow the instructions above, but split the stitch higher or lower than the middle (see Illus. 68).

Method of Stitching

Stitch one linear section of your design at a time. Illus. 63 was also worked in this way.

Finishing and Mounting

Complete this creation as described on page 18.

Another example of a *split-stitch* embroidery is the free-form landscape, done on rough cotton fabric, shown in Illus. 12. Various cords and jute were used in addition to a large variety of thick wools to create this striking stitchery.

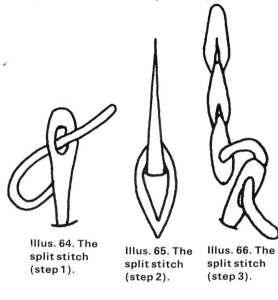

Illus. 64. The split stitch (step 1).

Illus. 65. The split stitch (step 2).

Illus. 66. The split stitch (step 3).

Illus. 67. Variation 1 of the split stitch.

Illus. 68. Variation 2 of the split stitch.

The Blanket Stitch

The *blanket stitch* was originally used for edging blankets. It is also known as the *buttonhole stitch* because if you sew the stitches very close together, you can use them to make buttonholes.

The *blanket stitch* is a versatile stitch which you can use as the basis for many other stitches. It is especially good for stitching abstract patterns, hills, mountains, grasses and flowers. It creates a raised and flat surface with both smooth and rough areas.

Planning the Design

Abstraction, described on page 29, was the method used to design the magnificent *blanket-stitch* landscape with a setting sun shown in Illus. 69 and color Illus. 23.

Preparing the Fabric

Monk's cloth was used for Illus. 69. The fabric was cut 4 inches (10 cm.) larger than the planned stitchery design, because a large wooden em-

Illus. 69. This landscape with a setting sun is an excellent example of how you can use just one stitch to create a unique "painting." This landscape is also shown in color Illus. 23.

broidery hoop held the piece while it was being stitched.

Stitching

Cut a 30-inch (75-cm.) length of yarn and knot it.

Blanket Stitch (Illus. 70 and 71)

Step 1: Bring the needle up from the back of the fabric onto the lower line.

Step 2: Insert the needle in position on the upper line, taking a straight downwards stitch with the thread under the needle point.

Step 3: Pull up the stitch to form a loop and repeat, bringing the needle up a short distance away on the lower line.

Variations

1. Follow the instructions above, but vary the length of each stitch (see Illus. 72).

2. Follow the instructions above, but vary the space between the stitches (see Illus. 73.)

Method of Stitching

This particular *blanket-stitch* piece was worked by stitching one section at a time. How you stitch yours depends, of course, on the design you have planned and the types of fabric and threads you have chosen.

Finishing and Mounting

Iron your completed stitchery. Then decide how to finish it. Color Illus. 23 shows this project mounted on a piece of heavy matboard. You can also use foam-core board here. Simply tape the

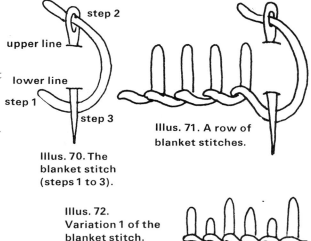

Illus. 70. The blanket stitch (steps 1 to 3).

Illus. 71. A row of blanket stitches.

Illus. 72. Variation 1 of the blanket stitch.

Illus. 73. Variation 2 of the blanket stitch.

stitchery around the back of the board. Then attach a pre-pasted picture hook to the back for hanging.

Illus. 69 shows this same stitchery in a wooden frame. Note the different effects you can achieve by the type of finishing you choose for your work.

Ready-made wooden frames come finished and unfinished in standard sizes. You must plan your stitchery and then mount it on stretchers that conform to these sizes before you begin working on it. If you choose an unfinished frame, you can varnish, stain, paint or antique it to complement your stitchery. Be sure to do this before you frame the stitchery.

The French Knot

The *French knot* is also known as the *French dot*, the *knotted stitch,* the *twisted knot* and the *wound stitch*. It produces a highly textured surface suitable for rough, coarse, hairy or flowered objects. Traditionally used for flowers because of this raised surface, the *French knot* can also be used for lines, borders, and other solid areas such as hair, flowering trees and animals with woolly coats.

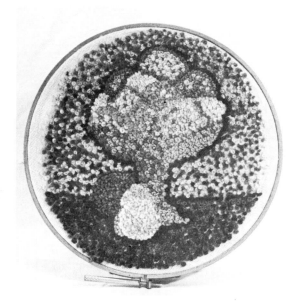

Illus. 74. The highly raised surface created by French knots is not only pleasing to look at, but is also fun to make. Hundreds of round, raised dots formed this charming still-life, which is also shown in color Illus. 24.

Planning the Design

A still-life of a bowl of fruit on a table, adapted by simplification—reducing the objects to their basic shapes (see page 18)—served as the pattern for the marvellously textured *French knot* stitchery in Illus. 74 and color Illus. 24.

Preparing the Fabric

The design for Illus. 74 was the exact size for the planned stitchery; therefore, scaling was not necessary. You may need to scale your design as described on page 14. When your design is the proper size, use the carbon-paper technique (see page 23) to transfer it to your fabric.

An even-weave wool fabric was chosen for the background for this stitchery. Because the design was in a circle, the artist used a wooden hoop.

If you plan to use this type of hoop, cut your fabric allowing a minimum of 3 extra inches (7.5 cm.) for a border all around to avoid fraying. Then place the fabric in the hoop, centering the hoop around the design. Tighten the tension on the hoop so that the fabric is taut.

Choosing the Thread

Realistic colors with some accent color added were chosen for Illus. 74. Yellows, greens, browns, oranges, purples and reds make up the color scheme. Use a variety of threads from cotton pearl to crewel and tapestry wool to emphasize the textured effects of the *French knot*. Use a length of thread 30 inches (75 cm.) long.

Stitching

French Knot (Illus. 75 and 76)

Step 1: Bring the needle up from the back of the fabric.

Step 2: Twist the thread around the needle twice and hold it taut close to the point.

Step 3: Insert the needle into the fabric as close to where it emerged as possible.

Step 4: Pull the needle through the fabric.

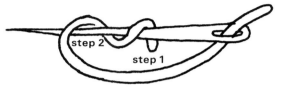

Illus. 75. The French knot (steps 1 and 2).

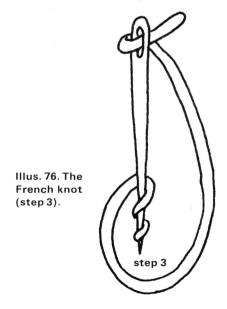

Illus. 76. The French knot (step 3).

Variation

Follow the instructions above, but vary the number of times you wind the thread around the needle (see Illus. 77).

Illus. 77. Variation of the French knot.

Method of Stitching

When you are making *French knots*, it is best to work one area at a time.

Finishing and Mounting

Because Illus. 74 was circular in shape, a circular frame was chosen to complete the project. A simple circular frame is a wooden hoop. Simply pull the remaining fabric to the back and tack it down.

Another more traditional way of finishing this piece is to frame it. Sometimes you can find an unusual, ornately carved or genuine antique frame at a flea market or antique shop. It is sometimes even worthwhile to buy a frame you particularly like and put it away until you have completed a stitchery that is suitable for it.

You have now learned 10 basic embroidery stitches and have seen many exciting projects using these stitches. See now what marvellous stitcheries *you* can create with your newly acquired skills.

Index

abstraction, 29–30, 44
anchoring stitch, 41
antique couching, 31
back stitch, 35, 43
bird design, 17, 42
blanket stitch, 24, 44–45
bowl of fruit design, 25, 46
burlap, 7, 34
buttonhole stitch, 44
carbon-paper transfer technique, 23, 27, 34, 40, 43, 46
chain stitch, 16, 40–41
chair design, 29, 30
chenille needle, 6
choosing the thread, 14, 21, 27, 31, 35, 38, 40, 43, 46
circular frame, 25, 47
close-up device, 12–13, 40
collage, 20–21, 34, 37–38
cords and twine, 9
cotton, 7, 27, 38
cotton thread, 8–9, 14, 19, 21, 35, 43, 46
couching, 25–30
crewel or embroidery needle, 6
crewel stitch, 34
cross stitch, 28, 37–39
dance rehearsal design, 18, 19
dressmaker's carbon paper, 23
fabrics, 7–8
fabric storage, 10
felt, 8
fern design, 11, 12, 13, 14, 15, 18
finishing and mounting, 15, 18–19, 23, 29–30, 32, 36, 39, 41, 43, 45, 47
floor frame, 7

foam-core board, 45
frames, 7, 23, 32, 36, 41, 45, 47
frames, embroidery, 7, 40
picture, 7
frames, metal, 32
frames, plastic, 23
frames, wood, 41, 45
free-form landscape design, 17, 43
French dot, 46
French knot, 25, 46–47
hoops, embroidery, 6–7, 31, 44, 46
hand-held, 6, 21
on a stand, 6–7
Janina stitch, 31
knotted stitch, 46
landscape with setting sun design, 24, 44
landscape with trees design, 32–33
letters design, 20
linen, 7, 21, 31, 37, 42
matboard, 45
materials, 5–9
monk's cloth, 40, 44
mountains and hills design, 16, 40
needles, 4, 6
no-frame method, 18
onion design, 25, 26
Oriental couching, 31
outline stitch, 34–36
planning the design, 11–13, 20–21, 26, 31, 34, 37, 40, 42, 44, 46
preparing the fabric, 13–15, 21, 27, 31, 34, 38, 40, 42–43, 44–45, 46
repetition, 26, 31
rose petals design, 31, 32

Roumanian stitch, 31–33
running stitch, 20–24
rustic outdoor scene, 34, 35
sampler, 37, 41
satin stitch, 11–19
scaling, 13–14, 38
scissors, 6
sea-scape design, 28, 39
sham satin stitch, 11
sharp needle, 6
silk, 7
silk thread, 9, 35
simplification, 18–19, 46
soft sculpture, 23–24
South Kensington stitch, 34
split stitch, 17, 42 –44
stalk stitch, 34
stem stitch, 34
stitching, 14–15, 21–23, 27–29, 31–32, 35–36, 38–39, 40–41, 43, 45, 47
storage, 5, 10
stretcher frame method, 14
stretcher strips, 7, 14, 18, 27, 34, 36, 38, 42
surface satin stitch, 11
tacking stitch, 27, 32
tapestry needle, 6
thimbles, 6
threads, 8–9
tissue-paper transfer technique, 21
tool box, 10
tools, 5–7
twisted stitch, 46
wood stripping, 36
wool, 7, 13, 46
wool thread, 9, 14, 21, 27, 31, 35, 40, 43, 46
wound stitch, 46